Camp Without Coolers or Stoves

Tasty Meals with Absolutely No Cooking!

Kick the Cooler Habit!

Lacey Anderson

Author of
Camp Cooking Without Coolers II

To inform me of errors, omissions or to share recipe modifications, please contact me at:

cookbook@nocoolers.com

Visit us at:

No Coolers Blog: **www.nocoolers.com**

Published Titles:
Camp Cooking WITHOUT Coolers II: Blueprint for Using Nonperishable Food
Camp WITHOUT Coolers or Stoves: Tasty Meals With Absolutely NO COOKING!

COMING SOON:
Camp Without Coolers: Fresh & Healthy Vegetarian
CWC: Quick & Easy Vegetarian
CWC: The Nomadic Vegetarian
CWC: 3-Week Plan, Grand Canyon Style

TABLE OF CONTENTS

INTRODUCTION 1

MENU 2

INGREDIENT NOTES 8

NO COOKING KITCHEN TECHNIQUES 14

BREAKFAST... 23

    Orange Julius Fruit Salad 23

    Homemade Peanut Butter Lara Bars 24

    Vanilla Blueberry Crunch.................................. 26

    Fruity-Nutty Bulgur.. 27

    Power Dates 29

    Apple Muesli 30

    Fruit Shake... 32

    Sweet and Sour Fruit Salad 33

    Breakfast Granola Balls 34

LUNCH 36

    Creamy Tuna Pockets 36

    Black Bean Wraps 38

    Eastern Hummus Wraps 39

    Spiced Jicama Sticks 41

    GORP Deluxe 42

    Savoury Three Bean Salad 43

    B&M Brown Bread Sandwiches 44

HAPPY HOUR DRINKS 45

    Tequila.. 45

    Margaritas 45

Simply Tasty Margarita 46
Neil's Authentic Margarita 46
Baja Bob's Sugar-Free Margarita 46
Pina Colada 47
Wine 47
Whiskey 47
APPETIZERS 48
Tostadas Picante 48
Multi-Grain Pesto Rounds............................... 49
Greek Platter 50
Hummus Dip with Vegetables and Crackers.... 51
Gazpacho 52
DINNER SALADS 53
Colourful Carrot Slaw..................................... 53
Broccoli Salad... 54
Carrot Ginger Slaw 55
Tangy Waldorf Salad 56
Chayote Slaw 57
MAIN ENTRÉES... 58
Chicken Spring Rolls with Peanut Sauce 58
Healthiest Chinese Chicken Salad 60
Traditional Chinese Chicken Salad................... 62
Chicken Verde Wrap....................................... 64
Summer Lentils.. 65
Mango Couscous with Creamed Salmon 66
Southwest Smorgasbord 68
DESSERTS.. 70
Marias Cookie Snacks.................................... 70

Dutch Almond Dates 71

Peach Leche Cake 72

No-fuss Cherry Cheesecake 73

Rum Balls 77

LOW-IMPACT CAMPING 79

ABOUT THE AUTHOR 83

THANK YOU 86

INTRODUCTION

This cookbook contains recipes that are easy to prepare and healthy. Even more importantly these recipes do not require coolers, ice, or cooking.

Yep, I said NO cooking!

My friend Keith, who happily bought the original version of Camp Cooking WITHOUT Coolers, was the inspiration for this no cooking version.

On a "demonstration" trip down the East Fork Carson River where I was showing how well you can eat using my recipes for delicious meals with lightweight, nonperishable ingredients, Keith was one of the enthusiastic participants. After sampling the Asian Couscous for lunch, which is very tasty and made without cooking, he asked if I could do an entire meal plan without cooking. I thought a bit about this challenge and decided that yes, indeed I could get together enough "no cooking" recipes to do a full meal plan (breakfast, lunch, appetizer, salad, main entrée, and dessert) where NONE of the meals required any cooking. This version of Camp Cooking WITHOUT Coolers is the result.

With this collection of recipes, you too can eat well without using a stove, fuel, charcoal, or other heat source; absolutely NO cooking! You don't need a Dutch oven, frying pan or cooking pots. You don't even have to boil water. Because no fuels are used that makes it Eco-Friendly too.

Here's to you Keith, thanks for the great idea!

MENU

The five day menu includes breakfast, lunch, and a themed multi-course dinner each day. Dinners start with happy hour where drinks and appetizers are served. Then the main entrée is served with salad and bread. Lastly, top the meal off with a delicious dessert. Use the 5-Day Menu in its entirety or pick and choose individual recipes to supplement your own recipe collection.

DAY 1

Breakfast

 Orange Julius Fruit Salad

 Homemade Peanut Butter Lara Bars

Lunch

 Creamy Tuna Pockets,

 Dried Wasabi Peas

 Apples

Dinner - Asian European Fusion

 <u>Drinks & Appetizer</u>

  Pina Colada

  Multi-Grain Pesto Rounds

Salad & Bread

Colorful Carrot Slaw

Ak-Mak Sesame Crackers

Main Entrée

Chicken Spring Rolls with Peanut Sauce
(vegetarian option)

Dessert

Marias Cookie Snacks

DAY 2

Breakfast

> Vanilla Blueberry Crunch
>
> Apple Slices

Lunch

> Black Bean Wraps
>
> Fresh Baby Carrots
>
> Flaxseed Chips

Dinner - World Market

> <u>Drinks & Appetizer</u>
>
>> Spit-Fire Cinnamon Whisky
>>
>> Hummus Dip with Vegetables and Crackers
>
> <u>Salad & Bread</u>
>
>> Broccoli Salad
>>
>> Naan or Flatbread
>
> <u>Main Entrée</u>
>
>> Chinese Chicken Salad (vegetarian option)
>
> <u>Dessert</u>
>
>> Dutch Almond Dates

DAY 3

Breakfast

Fruity-Nutty Bulgur

Power Dates

Lunch

Eastern Hummus Wrap

Spiced Jicama Sticks

GORP Deluxe

Dinner - Latin Fiesta

Drinks & Appetizer

Baja Bob's Margaritas

Tostidos Picante

Salad & Bread

Carrot Ginger Slaw

Rice Cakes

Main Entrée

Chicken Verde Wrap

Dessert

Peach Leche Cake

DAY 4

Breakfast

Apple Muesli

Fruit Shake

Lunch

Savory Three Bean Salad

B&M Brown Bread Sandwiches

Fresh or Dried Fruit

Dinner - Mediterranean Delight

<u>Drinks & Appetizer</u>

Sipping Tequila

Greek Platter

<u>Salad & Bread</u>

Tangy Waldorf Salad

Wheat Thins

<u>Main Entrée</u>

Mango Couscous with Creamed Salmon

<u>Dessert</u>

No Fuss Cherry Cheesecake

DAY 5

Breakfast

Sweet and Sour Fruit Salad

Breakfast Granola Balls

Lunch

Summer Lentils

Salami, Sardines and Crackers

Dried Fruits and Nut

Dinner - Savory Southwest

Drinks & Appetizer

Wine, Margaritas, whatever is left, finish it up!

Gazpacho

Salad

Chayote Slaw

Main Entrée

Southwest Smorgasbord

Dessert

Rum Balls

INGREDIENT NOTES

The primary source for ingredients will be your local supermarket, but international markets and health food stores are excellent places to shop as well. I have found lots of tasty affordable foods, like sprats (awesome little smoked fish), spring roll wrappers, rice noodles, and lots more at local international food markets. Health food stores are a good source of dehydrated fruits and vegetables, meatless entrees, grains, dairy substitutes, alternative noodles and more. Have fun exploring the shopping options in your neighborhood.

The recipe ingredients in this cookbook are, for the most part, readily available, yet some of the ingredients may be things that you are not familiar with in your general cooking. Here are descriptions of some of the ingredients found in my recipes, suggestions on where to find them in the supermarket aisle, and websites for the unusual food products. Keep in mind, if all else fails and you cannot find a product at your local grocer almost all the ingredients and food items can be ordered on Amazon.com.

Ancho Chili Powder is different than the typical chili powder. Ancho chilies have a milder, sweeter flavor than the American style chili powder. Look for ancho chili powder in the "International" aisle of your supermarket or at a local Mexican market.

B&M Brown Bread is a delicious tradition in many New England families. It is a mix of whole wheat and rye flour with molasses as the sweetener. It is a tasty bread that comes in a can, yep a can! There are two varieties: plain or with raisins (I love the raisin one).

This canned bread is generally found in the "Bean" aisle of supermarkets.
http://www.famousfoods.com/bmbrbrp.html

Bulgur - Bob's Red Mill brand quick cooking bulgur is my secret ingredient for the Fruity Nutty Bulgur recipe. Bob's quick cooking variety has been ground so that it is finer and thus reconstitutes without cooking. Look in the "natural foods" or "organic aisle" at your local grocer or at a local health food stores.
http://www.bobsredmill.com

Canned Cheddar Cheese - Bega brand is very good, I actually keep it in my home cupboard as well. It can be found online with a simple search, but the store Emergency Essentials seems to have the best price for smaller orders. http://beprepared.com/bega-canned-processed-cheese-7-05-oz.html

Chia Seeds are nutrient-dense seeds and an excellent source of vitamins, antioxidants, protein, Omega-3 fatty acids, calcium, iron and more! This seed has become a staple in many households, more and more local grocers are carrying them. This product can also be found in health food stores and larger supermarkets with a health food section.

Chayote is a wonderful vegetable. Chayote can be eaten raw or cooked. It will keep for long periods of time without refrigeration. It is a mild flavored vegetable that has a taste somewhere between a cucumber and an apple. It looks like a flattened green pear.

Crema - Find it in a can or small carton under the name Media Crema Table Cream. Crema is a delicious light cream. http://www.mexgrocer.com/2571.html

Flatbread is a Middle Eastern style bread, reminiscent of a very thick flour tortilla. Flatout is one of my favorite brands for its flavor and texture. This brand also has a history of keeping (no mold) for a week or more on my trips. Flour tortillas can be substituted for flatbread if you prefer. http://www.flatoutbread.com/

Freeze-dried Mangoes from Honeyville Farms are excellent quality freeze-dried fruit. Trader Joe's also carries small packets of freeze-dried fruits. If you have difficulty finding freeze-dried mangoes and you do not want to order online, there is an alternative. Freeze-dried mangoes can be replaced with dehydrated mangoes. Most grocery stores carry dehydrated mangoes. Honeyville - http://local.honeyvillegrain.com/ or Trader Joes http://www.traderjoes.com/

Frijoles Negro Refritos are refried black beans. They come in a handy pouch instead of a can. You can find them at Mexican markets, international markets, and some supermarkets. They have a delightful flavor and the pouch makes for easy opening and disposal of trash (no sharp can edges to deal with) The San Francisco brand is excellent.

Powdered Hummus - I keep powdered hummus in my home cupboards. It is easy to mix a batch up whenever I like. With the powdered (dried) variety I never have to worry about spoilage and the powdered variety is just as tasty as fresh! Powdered hummus can be found in most supermarkets and health food stores. Fantastic

Foods is my preferred brand.
http://www.fantasticworldfoods.com/

Jicama is a round, brown-skinned tuber vegetable. It has a neutral flavor is crisp and moist. The small to medium sized jicamas have the best texture and flavor. Jicama keeps well for long periods of time, if kept dry.

Kelp Noodles are a sea vegetable in an easy to eat raw noodle. Kelp noodles are fat-free, gluten free and very low in carbohydrates and calories. Available at health food stores. http://kelpnoodles.com/

Maple Syrup Powder can be found in many health food stores and some international markets. This is an excellent natural powdered sweetener.

Margarita Mix from Baja Bob's. The powdered margarita mix is fantastic! Some grocery stores and BevMo carry it. I like the "original" flavor the best. www.bajabob.com/

NIDO (powdered milk) -The key to good tasting powdered milk (like NIDO) is that it is dried whole milk, rather than skim or low fat milk. NIDO can be found in many supermarkets, Super Wal-Mart, and many international food stores.

Nutella is a hazelnut chocolate spread. Most supermarkets carry it; usually found along with peanut butter.

Parmesan Cheese made by Kraft works well for the No Coolers camp kitchen, but some people prefer a fresher cheese. Aged parmesan cheeses that are hard and contain less oils, fats and moisture will stay fresh the longest.

Pesto Paste is handy for the No Coolers camp kitchen. There are several brands out there, but the one I prefer is Napoleon. It is sold in most grocery stores. Look for pesto pastes that come in a really handy squeeze tube. http://www.napoleon-co.com/index.html

Pita Bread I can recommend Sara Lee. The plain white flour pita pockets keep the longest. I do not buy the whole wheat simply because it has gotten moldy in just a few days every time I have tried it. Tortillas and flat bread are tasty alternatives.

Sour Cream Powder - For the Mango Couscous with Creamed Salmon recipe you will need to order freeze-dried sour cream powder. The best tasting brand I have found is from Alpine Aire Foods. http://www.alpineaire.com/index.php?main_page=product_info&products_id=166

Spring Roll Skins are made from rice. Spring roll wrappers are low in calories and fat and high in protein. Good for a gluten-free diet because they are made from rice and tapioca flour, not wheat products. Be sure to buy the brands made from rice paper because they make the best raw wrap. Rice spring roll skins are soft and pliable once soaked in water.

Sun Dried Tomatoes. The California Sun Dry brand are the best. This brand has a pleasing moist and fresh texture with a rich tomato flavor. Other brands can be too salty. http://calsundrytomatoes.com

True Lime is 100% natural; it is made from fresh limes. Cold pressing and crystallizing the lemons locks in the great flavor and nutrients. http://truelemon.com/

Tuna - pouched albacore is better than canned for camping because there is no need to drain the tuna and there is no can to crush or sharp edges to deal with. I prefer albacore to the standard "light" tuna.

Vanilla Protein Powder can be found in many health food stores and some international markets. There are a lot of good tasting protein powders on the market, but lately I have been using Nature's Plus Energy Shake powder.

Yogurt Powder - This is a freeze-dried powder that makes the cream for the creamy tuna pockets recipe. Canned crema can be used in place of the yogurt powder.

Additional Sources For Dehydrated And Freeze-Dried Products

North Bay Trading website
http://www.northbaytrading.com/

Frontier Coop website
http://www.frontiercoop.com/

Harmony House website
http://www.harmonyhousefoods.com/

NO COOKING KITCHEN TECHNIQUES

Keeping Produce Fresh

Start with the freshest produce you can find; buy fresh produce directly from the farmer if possible. Purchase fruits and vegetables immediately before your trip and select the freshest produce without any bruising or discoloration. Do not purchase produce that is wilted or showing signs of age. Keep the produce dry and out of direct sunlight. Check for moisture daily and allow to air dry whenever possible.

DO NOT wash produce before packing; washing may introduce water born bacteria that can start the decomposition process. Take extra care in when packing produce for an extended trip. Fresh produce will last longer if it has a cushion wrap of some sort. You can cushion produce with a variety of materials: cloth towels, paper towels, newspaper, paper bags, etc. Wrapping will keep the produce from bruising; once wrapped, place in a hard shelled container such as a Vittle Vault (see resource section for where to find a Vittle Vault).

Fresh produce needs extra care while on your trip. Keep the food out of the full sun and move to the shade whenever possible. Remember to keep fruits and vegetables as dry as possible. Check the produce every day for moisture and condensation. If it does become damp, dry it, check for bad spots, and repackage the dry undamaged produce. Rewrap with new dry packing material. Check the produce every day and if any produce is bruised, over-ripe or beginning to mold, throw it out. The saying "it only takes one bad apple to spoil the whole barrel" holds true. Once something starts to spoil, everything it touches won't be far behind.

The weather will make a difference in how long produce stays fresh. Produce will keep in hot weather without being on ice, but it will need more attention than during cold weather. Likewise it is surprising how long produce will stay fresh and crisp in cooler weather (75 degrees and less) without too much fuss.

One final tidbit about keeping foods fresh: pay attention to the menu order while on the trip. Prepare the recipes that have the most perishable ingredients on the earlier days of the trip. Save the recipes that have no perishable items for the last days of your trip.

Produce Freshness and Storage Guidelines

One very important general rule for all produce – keep it dry! Check produce on a daily basis for wetness. If it does become damp, dry it off, check and remove bad spots and repackage the dry undamaged produce. Here are some general guidelines on how long produce can be stored without refrigeration.

Medjool Dates

>   Storage Length: Several months

Apples

>   Storage Length: up to1 month

>   Special Care: Tart apples (like Granny Smith) keep the longest. Does not store well with citrus because it will cause ripening sooner.

Citrus (oranges, lemons, limes)

> Storage Length: up to 1 month

> Special Care: Do not store with apples.

Green Cabbage

> Storage Length: up to 3 weeks

> Special Care: Wrap in towels or some sort of protective cover.

Jicama

> Storage Length: up to 3 weeks

> Special Care: Do not let moisture develop (jicama will mold if it gets wet)

English Cucumber

> Storage Length: up to 2 weeks

> Special Care: "English Cucumbers" wrapped in cellophane without bruises last the longest.

Carrots

> Storage Length: up to 2 weeks

> Special Care: Store with tops off.

Broccoli

> Storage Length: up to 5 days

Bell Pepper

> Storage Length: up to 5 days

> Special Care: Buy green bell peppers because the green ones will last the longest. Green peppers will begin to ripen and turn yellow, then red.

Romaine Lettuce

> Storage Length: up to 4 days

> Special Care: Unroll a paper towel roll, peel the lettuce leaves off of lettuce core and lay individual leaves on paper towels. Make sure the lettuce is dry. Reroll the paper back into the cylinder shape and place the leaves into green bags. See my website for a romaine lettuce storage tutorial https://www.youtube.com/watch?v=IaD3oO7b HTE

Green Onions

> Storage Length: up to 3 days

How to Choose the Best Produce

Apples

> Choose apples that have a full color, no discoloration, is a round rather than an elongated shape.

> Do not purchase if apples are soft, discolored, or mushy to touch.

Citrus

> Choose fruit that is heavy, firm, and with a smooth texture.

> Do not purchase if citrus has a rough texture, is light weight, dull, dry, or spongy.

Cabbage

Choose a head that has tight leaves, a solid heft. Larger sizes tend to have a milder flavor.

Do not purchase if cabbage is wilted, brown, or excessively torn.

Carrots

Choose carrots that are bright orange, smooth, and firm.

Do not purchase if carrots have a rough texture, green roots, wilted, or are rubbery with soft spots.

Jicama

Choose jicama that is a small to medium size.

Do not purchase if jicama is dull or blemished.

Broccoli

Choose broccoli that is firm, has a deep green color, and has closed compact florets.

Do not purchase if broccoli has a yellow color, open florets, is soft, slippery, rubbery, or has water-spots.

Bell Pepper

Choose peppers that are: bright, firm, and have glossy skin.

Do not purchase if the pepper has soft spots, is dull, or shriveled.

Romaine Lettuce

> Choose lettuce that is: dark green with firmly attached leaves.

> Do not purchase if it has a brown or mushy core.

Green Onions

> Choose bunches that have crisp bright green tops with a firm white base.

> Do not purchase if there are many with mushy or droopy tops.

Freeze-Dried Versus Dehydrated Foods

Freeze-dried and dehydrated foods are very different from each other with very different cooking directions and preparation techniques. They are not normally interchangeable in recipes. "No cooking" recipes will turn out best if you use the exact ingredients listed in the ingredient list. Pay special attention when the recipe calls for something that is fresh, dehydrated or freeze-dried.

Freeze-dried - The freeze drying process is quite amazing. Fresh produce is put into a large vacuum and brought to an extremely low temperature. A vacuum is applied and the moisture in the fruit is removed. This process allows for up to 97% of the liquid volume to be removed, much more than dehydrating. The end result is a product that is crisp and light with all of the nutritional value. Cell structure remains intact, which results in excellent retention of flavor, color, shape, and nutritional value.

Freeze dried food can be eaten as is, or rehydrated quickly. Freeze-dried foods are good for the quick meals; the ones that do not require much cooking. Freeze-dried products rehydrate very quickly. If freeze-dried items are cooked for too long they may turn to mush.

Dehydrated (dried) - Dehydrated vegetables and fruits are made by subjecting vegetables and fruit to heat, resulting in water evaporation. The physical size of the vegetables are reduced when air dried. When cooked, these vegetables rehydrate nicely and often remain intact. Dehydrated foods are better for the meals that require a longer cooking time because they maintain their form and texture even after a long simmer. In fact, if the dehydrated food does not cook long enough it may be tough or chewy.

Cheese in the "No Coolers" Kitchen

Cheeses that are hard and contain less oils, fats and moisture will stay fresh the longest. Hard cheeses encased in wax are also a good choice. Generally speaking, soft cheeses will last for one or two days if you are in a cool environment. If you want cheese to last longer, opt for a hard cheese such as Gruyere or aged Gouda which will last for a week or so. I have also had good luck with string and mozzarella cheese, they seem to keep well without a cooler for a week or so. Parmesan cheeses also keep well; I have had parmesan last for weeks without a cooler or refrigeration. Of course there is always Kraft brand dried parmesan that will last for weeks.

The oils from some cheeses may separate leaving an oily film on the outside - this usually happens with softer cheeses. Enzymes and bacteria occur naturally in cheese and need to be exposed to air and moisture to keep the cheese fresh and flavorful. For this reason, fresh cheese should not be stored in an airtight wrapping, such as plastic wrap or a sandwich bag.

Wrap cheeses in wax or parchment paper, layers of cheesecloth or a plain brown paper bag. Secure the wrapping with a rubber band and store the cheese in a cool container. Give cheeses the same special treatment as produce: keep out of full sun, store in a cool spot, and keep them dry.

If your cheese begins to mold, you can salvage it. Make a cut about half inch below the mold to make sure it has been entirely removed and discard the moldy pieces. The remaining cheese will be fine.

Canned cheese is also an option – really! Bega is the brand I use and like very much, so much so that I keep it stocked in my home kitchen. Canned cheese can be ordered online, see the Ingredients Notes section for where to order.

Kitchen Utensils

These are the kitchen utensils needed for recipe preparation in this cookbook.

> Mixing/Serving bowls of various sizes
>
> Mixing spoons – slotted and solid
>
> Measuring cup – standard ¼, ⅓, ½, and 1 cup sizes
>
> Measuring spoons – standard ¼ and ½ teaspoon and Tablespoon sizes
>
> Serving spoons
>
> Sharp knives for cutting/chopping produce

Cutting board

Kitchen scissors

Serving plate

Grater

Whisk

Zip top freezer bags – variety of sizes from 1 quart to 2 gallon

Roll of paper towels

Very sturdy stiff fork (especially if you're making the homemade Lara Bars)

Thin gloves (for mixing food by hand)

Kitchen and Packing Products

Big Basin Water Container can be purchased online from NRS. The "Big Basin Water Container" is for the "Bucket Refrigerator" system. These Big Basin Collapsible Containers are handy for dish washing and many other uses too. http://www.nrsweb.com/shop/product.asp?pfid=2051

Vittle Vaults are used in place of heavy ammo cans and metal storage boxes. They are durable, lightweight, and air tight. You can find these handy containers at most pet stores. http://www.petsmart.com/

BREAKFAST

Orange Julius Fruit Salad

You can choose your own favorite combination of fruits and it will taste good with the "Orange Julius" sauce, but I prefer to stick with mostly citrus fruits and bananas.

Makes 4 Servings

> 6 oranges or a citrus combo of oranges, mandarins, tangelos, etc.
>
> 2 or 3 oranges, juiced (you'll want about ⅔ of a cup)
>
> 4 bananas
>
> 4 heaping Tablespoons (or more) vanilla flavored protein powder
>
> ¼ cup (or more) slivered almonds
>
> ⅓ cup chia seeds
>
> ¼ cup (or so) of granola

Make the sauce first: Juice two or three oranges. Stir in the vanilla protein powder, mix until all lumps are gone, set aside.

Cut-up all the remaining fruit into bite-sized pieces and mix. Pour the juice mixture over the fruit. Top the mixture with slivered almonds, chia seeds, and granola.

Homemade Peanut Butter Lara Bars

Healthy energy bars made with two basic ingredient, dates and nuts!

Makes Approximately 8 Balls or 4 Small Bars

Balls

> ½ cup Medjool dates (pitted whole dates)
>
> ¼ cup cashews
>
> ¼ cup peanuts
>
> 1 Tablespoon peanut butter
>
> ¼ tsp ground cinnamon

Coating (optional)

> 1 Tablespoon powdered sugar
>
> 1 Tablespoon cocoa
>
> ½ Tablespoon chia seeds
>
> ½ Tablespoon protein powder

At Home: add cashews and peanuts to a food processor and pulse until chopped fairly small (small chunks, you want texture not flour). Place in a baggie to have the finely chopped nuts ready for use in camp.

In Camp: soak the dates in a bowl of water for 15 minutes. While the fruit is soaking, place the nuts in a bowl and add peanut butter and cinnamon. Mix well with a sturdy fork.

Thinly coat a pair of scissor blades with oil (dip a paper towel in a little oil and carefully rub along scissor blades). Hands get dirty while camping, so I suggest when using your hands for mixing and snipping dates you wear kitchen gloves. With the scissors, snip the dates into little pieces and drop into nut mixture. Use the sturdy fork (or your gloved hands) to mash and blend the mixture well. Use your gloved hands to shape the mixture into 1 inch balls or small bars.

Optional Coating: mix the coating ingredients in a small bowl. Drop the balls/bars in the coating mix, roll around to coat all sides, dust off and place on serving plate.

Vanilla Blueberry Crunch

I like this cereal so much; I have it at home too!

Makes 4 Servings

> 1 cup granola
>
> 1 cup Grape-Nuts cereal
>
> 2 Tablespoons dried cranberries
>
> 1 cup freeze dried blueberries
>
> 5 Tablespoons almonds slivered or chopped
>
> 2 Tablespoons hazelnuts chopped
>
> 6 Tablespoons macadamia nuts chopped
>
> 3 teaspoons vanilla powder
>
> 4 Tablespoons chia seeds (optional)
>
> 4 to 6 Tablespoons vanilla protein powder (optional)
>
> 6 Tablespoons whole milk powder (NIDO is the best)

At Home: Mix all dry ingredients (except the milk powder) and place in a sturdy bag (I use plastic freezer bags).

In Camp: Rehydrate the powdered milk in 2 cups of water. Serve the milk on the side.

* Freeze dried blueberries are good, but fresh are even better. If you get fresh berries do not add them to the mix, rather have them on the side with the milk.

Fruity-Nutty Bulgur

Prepare this recipe the night before you are planning to eat it and wake up to a "cooked" meal in the morning

Makes 8 Servings

> 2 ¼ cups quick cooking bulgur
>
> 6 Tablespoons dried cranberries
>
> 1 ½ cups freeze dried blueberries
>
> ½ cup freeze dried orange segments crushed to a powder
>
> 4 ½ cups of water
>
> 1 cup of freeze dried orange segments
>
> 1 ½ cups chopped walnut
>
> ¼ cup sesame seeds
>
> 6 Tablespoons whole milk powder (NIDO is the best) optional

Night Before Preparation: In a gallon size baggie or large pot, combine bulgur, cranberries, ½ cup blueberries, ½ cup powdered orange and water. Let this mixture sit overnight.

Morning Preparation: add walnuts and sesame seeds to the bulgur mixture that was prepared the night before, mix all together.

Before serving, set out the remaining 1 cup of orange segments and remaining 1 cup of blueberries, to be used for topping. Reconstitute the milk, if desired as an optional topping too (pour about ½ cup milk over a 1 cup serving of bulgur).

* The bulgur does not need milk, but I prefer it with milk. So if desired, rehydrate the milk powder (3 Tablespoons NIDO powder for every cup of water)

* Please read the preparation directions very carefully before making this breakfast. The directions are detailed and specific. If directions are not followed exactly the cereal may not come out right.

Power Dates

Dates are nature's perfect food, packed with vitamins, minerals, and flavor.

Makes 4 Servings

>16 large Medjool dates
>
>½ cup peanut butter
>
>¼ cup instant milk powder
>
>1 Tablespoon brown sugar
>
>½ Tablespoon honey (optional)
>
>2 Tablespoons slivered almonds
>
>2 Tablespoons oat bran
>
>1 teaspoon chia seeds (optional)
>
>Plus a little water – maybe

Prepare Dates: Cut open dates and remove seed, set aside.

Prepare Filling: Mix everything except the dates. It will be a stiff mixture, if it needs to be a little softer, add water a little at a time.

Fill dates with filling mixture. For serving presentation, lay them out on a plate in a pleasing pattern or cut the dates into about 3 pieces per date for an appetizing jelly-roll look.

Apple Muesli

Muesli is very easy to prepare, but it needs to sit for an hour. The camp cook should prepare it first thing in the morning. I suggest that everyone enjoy a cup of coffee or tea, pack up their personal camp items, go fishing, hiking, or just relax for an hour while the breakfast "cooks" and then come back to a tasty meal.

Makes 4 Servings

¼ cup NIDO (instant dry milk powder)

1 teaspoon cinnamon

½ teaspoon nutmeg

1 Tablespoon brown sugar

2 cups water

2 cups (9 oz.) Bob's Red Mill Muesli

2 Tablespoons raisins

¼ cup chia seeds (optional)

1 small fresh apple (optional, but highly recommended)

½ cup freeze dried blueberries (optional, but highly recommended)

Pour NIDO, cinnamon, nutmeg, brown sugar, into the water and stir. Add cereal, raisins and optional chia seeds, mix. Let sit for 1 hour and serve.

Just before serving, chop up fresh apple. Set out the blueberries. The fruits are toppings for individual servings.

*   You may be tempted to prepare Apple Muesli the night before and let it sit overnight, but I cannot recommend doing that. I have been told Europeans prepare their muesli the night before and let it sit overnight to eat in the morning. I tried that and it was too soggy for my taste.

Fruit Shake

You can use your favorite freeze dried fruit for this, but freeze dried oranges make an excellent fruit shake and they crush easily into a powder for mixing.

Makes 2 Servings

> 5 Tablespoons instant milk powder (only use NIDO or other whole milk powder)
>
> ½ cup freeze dried fruit (oranges are great), crushed
>
> 1 Tablespoon vanilla powder
>
> 1 Tablespoon maple powder
>
> 2 cups water (freshly filtered from a cold stream or river)

Add all ingredients to the water in bottle that has a tight, securely fitting lid. Shake, shake, shake, very hard for a few minutes, until powders are completely mixed and dissolved.

> * You will need to crush the freeze dried fruit; it is really easy. Place fruit in a tough (freezer) zip lock bag. Take a rolling pen or any hard round utensil (a Nalgene bottle works too), roll over and crush the bag.

Sweet and Sour Fruit Salad

For no-mess preparation and easy clean-up, mix everything in a large zip top freezer bag.

Makes 4 Servings

> 1 (15 oz) can mandarin orange segments in light syrup
>
> 1 lemon
>
> 1/4 cup raisins
>
> 1/4 cup walnuts, chopped
>
> 2 apples

Chop the apples, open and drain the mandarin oranges.

In a bowl mix the fruit with raisins and juice from the lemon. Add the walnuts.

Breakfast Granola Balls

All the flavors and texture blend perfectly if you make these ball the night before, but you may have to guard them from being eaten up that evening once everyone discovers how good they are!

Makes About A Dozen Balls

Ball Mixture

> ¼ cup peanut butter
>
> 2 Tablespoons maple syrup
>
> 2 Tablespoons apple juice (or other fruit juice)
>
> 1 ½ cups granola
>
> 1 Tablespoon or a little more of powdered milk (NIDO)
>
> ¼ cup carob or chocolate chips (optional)

Coating (optional)

> ¼ cup finely crushed peanuts or other nuts (optional)
>
> 1 Tablespoons NIDO (optional)
>
> 1 Tablespoons chia seeds (optional)

Combine the peanut butter, maple syrup, and juice in a bowl and use a fork to mix until well blended. Stir in the granola and mix well. Add the powdered milk and mix until mixture sticks together. Add in optional chocolate chips. Use your hands to roll the mixture into 1-inch balls and arrange on a plate

Optional coating: place the powdered milk, chia and sunflower seeds in a bowl and stir. Drop the balls into mixture to coat outside. Remove and place on a serving plate.

LUNCH

Creamy Tuna Pockets

A flavorful twist on traditional mayonaise based tuna sandwiches. Excellent served with dried wasabi peas and fresh apples.

Makes 4 To 6 Servings

> 2 ½ cups water
>
> 1 cup olive oil
>
> 1 cup julienne cut sun-dried tomatoes
>
> ½ cup diced or minced dehydrated onion
>
> 1 Tablespoon minced dehydrated garlic
>
> ⅓ to ½ cup dried basil
>
> 2 teaspoons ground black pepper
>
> 1 teaspoon salt
>
> 10 oz. pouched Albacore tuna (in water)
>
> 8 oz. string cheese in individual packs
>
> ½ cup yogurt powder
>
> 4 to 6 white flour pita bread, tortillas, or flat bread (Flatout brand is good)
>
> Fresh cabbage or lettuce (optional)
>
> 1 gallon zip top freezer bag (optional)

Add water, oil, vegetables, and spice to the freezer bag. Seal tightly and let sit to rehydrate for 15 to 30 minutes.

Slice the string cheese into little rounds and add it to the vegetables. Add the pouched tuna (liquid and all) to the rehydrated vegetables and spices in the bag. Add the yogurt powder and zip close top securely. Knead gently until well mixed.

To serve: if using the fresh lettuce or cabbage, do not put it in the wrap, rather, place it on the outside of the bread. The cabbage or vegetable leaf works as the very outside layer, it catches the juice, making the sandwich less messy, and tastes good too.

* The yogurt powder gives this recipe the creaminess, but Crema (in a can) can be substituted for the powdered yogurt.

* Save yourself the hassle of cleaning up bowls by preparing this meal in a large zip lock freezer bag.

Dried Wasabi Peas

Dried Wasabi Peas are dried green peas with a spicy wasabi coating. They have a crunchy texture with a spicy kick. They are a good source of protein (6 g per 1 ounce).

Black Bean Wraps

Super easy and very tasty! Serve these wraps with flaxseed corn chips and fresh baby carrots

Makes 4 Servings

> 1 ½ cups (14 oz pouch) Frijoles Negras Refritos in a pouch
>
> 1 ¼ cups grated parmesan cheese
>
> ½ cup sun-dried tomatoes
>
> 1 package taco sized flour tortillas

To assemble the wraps: Spread about ¼ cup of beans, 3 Tablespoons of cheese and 2 Tablespoons of tomatoes per tortilla. Roll them up jelly roll style, cut in half and serve.

Flaxseed Corn Chips

Flaxseed Corn Chips are a flavorful and health conscious chip to accompany the black bean wrap and jicama stick lunch.

Eastern Hummus Wraps

The Eastern Hummus Wraps are good served with the Spiced Jicama Sticks and GORP Deluxe (recipes below).

Makes 1 ½ Cups Hummus, about 4 Servings

> ¾ cups instant hummus
>
> ¼ teaspoon mild curry powder
>
> ¼ teaspoon ginger powder
>
> ¾ cup freeze dried mangoes
>
> 2 Tablespoons olive oil
>
> 1 cup water
>
> 1 large jicama
>
> 1 cucumber
>
> 1 package of Flatbread (large tortillas work too)

Chop up about ¼ cup of jicama into small pieces (save the rest of the jicama for the Spiced Jicama Sticks recipe), chop up about ¼ cup of cucumber (slice the rest of the cucumber into rounds to serve on the side).

Place the dry ingredients into the zip top bag, add the water, oil, and chopped vegetables. Squeeze out any excess air and securely close the bag top, then very carefully knead to blend all ingredients.

If you would like hummus with a thinner consistency, very slowly knead in more water.

Spread the hummus on the bread and roll (depending on the typed of bread you have). Serve with extra cucumbers on the side and the Spiced Jicama Sticks (recipe below).

* Freeze-dried Mangoes - If it is difficult to find freeze-dried mangoes and you do not want to order online, freeze-dried mangoes can be replaced with dehydrated mangoes, which most grocery stores carry. For dehydrated mangoes use only ⅔ cup, chopped.

* For a no-mess preparation and clean-up mix everything in a gallon size durable zip top freezer bag, otherwise use a bowl.

Spiced Jicama Sticks

This is a popular food in Mexico. Street vendors in every city sell this yummy vegetable topped with lime and spices!

Makes 4 Servings

> 1 or 2 small to medium jicama
>
> 2 or 3 lemons or limes
>
> ¼ to ½ teaspoon paprika (mild), ancho chili powder (medium), cayenne pepper (hot), or any combination of spices you prefer
>
> Pinch of salt

Cut jicama into julienne strips (like french fries). Squeeze the juice of the lemon or lime over the jicama and sprinkle lightly with your choice of spice (paprika, ancho chili powder, or cayenne pepper) and a pinch of salt.

GORP Deluxe

GORP is an acronym for "good old raisins and peanuts". This deluxe mix takes GORP up to the next level of yumminess!

Makes 4 Servings

> 1 cup dark chocolate chips or bars chopped into small pieces
>
> ¾ cup dehydrated cranberries or raisins
>
> 1 cup dehydrated blueberries
>
> 1 cup slivered almonds
>
> 1 cup macadamia nuts chopped into small pieces

At Home: place in a heavy duty plastic bag and mix.

Savoury Three Bean Salad

This is a traditional bean salad served in my family from my childhood. B&M Brown Bread Sandwiches and fresh or dried fruit is a perfect combination for lunch.

Makes 4 Servings

> 16 ounce can cut green beans, drained
>
> 16 ounce cut wax beans, drained
>
> 15 ounce kidney beans, drained
>
> 1 cup chopped green pepper (optional)
>
> 3 Tablespoons sugar
>
> ½ cup vinegar
>
> ⅓ cup olive oil
>
> 1 teaspoon salt
>
> ¼ teaspoon pepper
>
> ½ cup 100% grated parmesan cheese (Kraft)

In large bowl, combine all ingredients (except parmesan cheese) and mix well. Set out the cheese as a topping.

* For no-mess preparation and easy clean-up, mix everything in a gallon size durable zip top freezer bag, otherwise use a bowl.

B&M Brown Bread Sandwiches

Canned bread? YES, you'll love this healthy traditional brown bread!

Makes 8 Open Faced Sandwiches

>   1 can B&M Brown Bread
>
>   1 cup (or so) of peanut butter
>
>   1 to 2 bananas (optional)

Open the B&M can on both ends with a can opener; bread can be pushed out of one side using the lid on the other. Cut bread into 8 rounds and spread about 2 Tablespoons of peanut butter on each round. Serve open faced with the optional banana slice.

HAPPY HOUR DRINKS

Tequila

Only use the best for sipping and shots, margaritas can be made with almost any variety.

Silver (or Blanco) tequila is un-aged and has a strong agave flavor; it is usually clear. Reposado ("restful") tequila is aged in oak barrels from 2 months to a year; the color is usually golden. Anejo is aged in oak barrels for over a year (2 years for double anejo) giving a light brown color and more complex taste.

My Favorite Sipping Tequilas (you can see I like anejos):

>Seleccion 1146 anejo

>Pueblo Viejo Orgullo anejo

>El Diamante Del Cielo anejo - extremely tasty, if you can find it send me a bottle!

>Gran Centenario anejo - a reasonably-priced, yet very good anejo

>Sauza Conmemorativo anejo

Margaritas

Margaritas can be made with any tequila, but "top shelf" margaritas usually use a reposado or anejo, although a good silver can make a fantastic margarita.

Costco (Kirkland) silver is pretty good for sipping and makes great margaritas. Sauza Hornitos also makes good margaritas. I am not a fan of Cuervo Gold or really cheap tequilas, even in my margaritas.

Simply Tasty Margarita

> 3 oz. Simply Limeade
>
> 1 to 1.5 oz. tequila
>
> Juice of 1 or 2 fresh limes.

Neil's Authentic Margarita

A less sweet and more authentic Mexican margarita uses all fresh lime juice, tequila, and agave nectar to sweeten to your taste.

Baja Bob's Sugar-Free Margarita

For an easy lightweight and non-perishable recipe, pack some of Baja Bob's sugar-free margarita mix (powder), mix it with water in camp, and follow the Simply Tasty Margarita recipe above using the mix instead of Limeade and adding 1 or 2 packages of True Lime powder to improve the flavor by adding tartness.

Pina Colada

Pina Coladas are easy to make. I have had good canned varieties (there are a lot to choose from in the market) For canned pina coladas all you need do is open the can, pour Pina Colada mix into container, and add the amount of rum you like. I have also experimented with canned coconut milk, pineapple juice, and rum. The ratio of coconut milk to pineapple juice is an individual taste.

Wine

Everyone has their own favorites, from boxes to aged vintages. Some of my favorite affordable wines are Barefoot Cellars Pinot Grigio, Columbia Crest Merlot and Cabernet, Windwalker Merlot. These named brands come in glass containers. For river transport I recommend never taking glass containers; you will need to pour the contents into a plastic bottle. To solve this problem I often just take boxed wine.

Whiskey

Not much of a whiskey drinker (prefer tequila) but on a recent river trip I had a few shots of Fireball Cinnamon Whiskey and really liked it. Whiskey aficionados I'm sure will have a preferred brand for shots.

APPETIZERS

Tostadas Picante

Cooks should grab one before they are set out for the group because they are so flavorful the tostadas get gobbled up immediately!

Makes 4 Servings

> 1 package Tostidos brand (or other) tostada rounds
>
> 1 pouch of Frijoles Refritos (refried beans)
>
> 1 can Crema
>
> 1 can Jalapenos sliced Rajas (I prefer Herdez brand)

Spread about 2 Tablespoons of beans on tostada. Top with a rajas peppers, carrots, and onions. Place prepared tostadas on serving plate and pour crema on top.

Multi-Grain Pesto Rounds

Quick, easy and delicious!

Makes 4 Servings

> 5 ounces (or so) crackers of your choice
>
> 10 ounces (or so) of fresh parmesan cheese
>
> Small tube of pesto paste (Napoleon or other pesto in a tube)

Slice cheese, place on cracker, and drizzle pesto on top.

Greek Platter

A Greek platter is a sampler plate of Greek food delights such as olives, Dolmas, salami, cheese and crackers.

Makes 4 Servings

> 5 ounces (or so) crackers of your choice
>
> 8 ounces (or so) cheese (see cheese section for suggestions)
>
> 8 ounces (or so) of sliced salami
>
> Small package of sun-dried tomatoes (California Sun Dry brand is the best)
>
> 1 small can Dolmas (stuffed grape leaves)
>
> Small foil (pouch) green olives

Arrange everything attractively on a plate.

Hummus Dip with Vegetables and Crackers

Powdered hummus has an excellent texture and flavor once reconstituted. I love it!

Makes 4 Servings

> 1 cup powdered hummus
>
> 2 to 3 Tablespoons olive oil (optional)
>
> 1 cup water
>
> 1 lemon (optional)
>
> 3 to 4 cups vegetables
>
> 2 to 3 cups crackers of your choice

Mix dry hummus, cold water (start with 1 cup of water and slowly add more if needed) with olive oil (optional) until it becomes a spreadable paste. Add squeezed lemon juice or leave it plain. Use a hummus to water ratio of 1 to 1 for a thicker consistency or increase the water for a creamier consistency, depending on how you like it. Set out crackers and vegetables for dipping into hummus.

* For no-mess preparation and clean-up, mix everything in a gallon size zip top freezer bag, otherwise prepare in a bowl.

Gazpacho

This quick and easy "soup" goes together in a flash!

Makes 4 Hearty Appetizer Servings

> 1 (14.5-ounce) can diced tomatoes, finely chopped
>
> 1 (4-ounce) can chopped spicy green chilies, drained
>
> 1 garlic clove, finely minced
>
> 1 Tablespoon dehydrated minced shallots
>
> 1 Tablespoon red wine vinegar
>
> 2 Tablespoons olive oil
>
> 2 (11.5 ounce) V8 Spicy Hot Vegetable Juice
>
> 1 (14.5 ounce) garbanzo beans
>
> 1 teaspoon dehydrated parsley
>
> 1 teaspoon Tabasco sauce (optional)
>
> Oyster crackers (optional)
>
> 1 or 2 avocados (optional)

Combine all of the ingredients in a large bowl and mix. Divide soup between 4 serving bowls. Cut avocado into large pieces and place on top of each individual soup bowl.

Set out Oyster crackers for a topping. Pass Tabasco at the table for those who like an extra jolt of heat.

DINNER SALADS

Colourful Carrot Slaw

Serve whole wheat Ak-Mak sesame crackers alongside.

Makes 2 To 3 Servings

> 2 carrots, grated
>
> 1 orange
>
> 1 Tablespoon sunflower seeds
>
> 1 Tablespoon pumpkin seeds
>
> ½ Tablespoon sesame seeds
>
> ½ Tablespoon chia seeds
>
> 1 teaspoon agave nectar

Peel and section the orange. Squeeze about ¼ of the orange (juice) over the grated carrots. Slice up the rest of the orange and add to carrots. Add the seeds and agave nectar, mix well.

Broccoli Salad

Sweet and sour, healty and tasty. I like it best served with Naan or Flatbread!

Makes 3 To 4 Servings

> 2 cups (about ½ lb) broccoli, chopped into small pieces
>
> ¼ cup cashews, chopped
>
> ¼ cup red onion, minced
>
> ¼ cup mayonnaise
>
> 2 to 3 Tablespoons fresh squeezed lemon juice, to taste
>
> 1 Tablespoon agave nectar or sweetener of your choice
>
> 2 Tablespoons dehydrated currents
>
> ½ cup sunflower seeds
>
> Salt & Pepper to taste

Chop off about ½ inch off the bottom of the broccoli stem and toss out. Cut up the rest of the broccoli into small pieces place in mixing container. Add everything else and stir until broccoli is coated. Add salt and pepper to taste.

* Mayonnaise - Important! Throw out leftover mayonnaise because once opened it will quickly go bad without refrigeration. Buy a small container of mayonnaise because the unused portion should be thrown out.

54

Carrot Ginger Slaw

Exotic blend of sweet and spicy!

Makes 3 To 4 Servings

2 ½ medium sized carrots, grated

1 cup red cabbage, shredded

½ cup raisins

3 Tablespoons sunflower seeds

3 Tablespoons pumpkin seeds

1 ½ teaspoons maple sugar powder (or honey or sugar)

1 Tablespoon lemon juice (about 1 medium sized lemon)

½ Tablespoon fresh ginger (about a couple inches long), grated

2 Tablespoons olive oil

Dash of salt

Grate carrots and shred the cabbage, place in mixing bowl and add the raisins and seeds. In a separate bowl mix the powdered maple, lemon juice, grated ginger, olive oil, and a dash of salt. Pour liquid over slaw and toss.

Tangy Waldorf Salad

The addition of jicama, ginger, garlic, and lemon juice make for a tart alternative to the traditional Waldorf. Serve with wheat thins.

Makes 4 Servings

　　2 carrots, shredded (about ½ cup)

　　1 small jicama or chayote, chopped (about 1 cup)

　　1 apple, chopped

　　1 inch piece of ginger, minced

　　1 clove garlic, minced

　　1 large lemon, juiced

　　¼ teaspoon salt

　　1 Tablespoon olive oil

　　1 Tablespoon agave nectar

　　¼ cup raisins

　　1 Tablespoon sesame seeds

　　½ cup sunflower seeds

In a large container mix all ingredients and serve.

Chayote Slaw

Chayote's are a vegetable that reminds me of a cross between and pear and a cucumber. Popular in Mexico and easy to find in the markets. They are extrely handy in the no coolers kitchen because they keep well and can be eaten fried, baked, boiled, or raw!

Makes 4 Servings

> 2 fresh chayotes
>
> 2 heaping teaspoons fresh ginger, minced
>
> 2 Tablespoons fresh red onion, chopped
>
> 2 Tablespoons oil
>
> 3 Tablespoons white vinegar
>
> 1 ½ teaspoons sugar

Peel and grate the chayote. Add the ginger and mix.

In a separate bowl, combine the oil, vinegar, and sugar, whisk it to emulsify until it is a whitish color. Pour the emulsified liquid over the vegetables, stir and serve.

MAIN ENTRÉES

Chicken Spring Rolls with Peanut Sauce

These are so good I eat them at home on a regular basis when I have the craving for fresh Asian cuisine!

Makes About A Dozen Rolls (4 Servings)

Sauce Ingredients:

⅓ cup water

5 packets True Lime

1 teaspoon garlic powder

1 ½ Tablespoons soy sauce

1 ½ Tablespoons sugar

3 Tablespoons smooth peanut butter

1 teaspoon powdered ginger

¼ teaspoon red pepper flakes

¼ cup vegetable oil

Filling Ingredients:

½ small green cabbage (about 3 cups shredded)

6 medium carrots (about 1 ½ cups grated)

½ red pepper (about 1 cup sliced very thin)

½ small red onion (about ½ cup sliced very thin)

⅔ cup chopped peanuts

20 to 24 oz canned chicken

12 oz package Spring Rolls Skin

Prepare the Sauce: Mix ⅓ cup water and True Lime. Add all the sauce ingredients and whisk well to make a smooth sauce. This will take a lot of whisking to combine and emulsify until it is smooth. It is emulsified once the oil and water do not separate.

Prepare the Filling: Mix all the vegetables, stir well. Add about ¼ cup of sauce (save the rest for dipping), chicken and peanuts, toss gently.

Prepare the Rolls: To soften the spring roll skins, submerge individual rice papers in a plate of shallow water a few seconds just to soften, one at a time. It will take about 30 to 45 seconds to soften skin. Do not over soak or the rice paper will start to disintegrate. Gently remove fill the softened skin with about ½ cup of filling, pour 1 Tablespoon of sauce onto the filling and roll. Note that it is important to apply a little pressure, as you roll, to ensure that the roll is firm and tight. Do not have rolls touching each other because they will stick.

Let the rolls sit for 10 minutes or more to dry out a little.

Serve with the remaining dipping sauce.

Healthiest Chinese Chicken Salad

This is a healthy and easy raw alternative to the ramen noodles in Traditional Chinese Chicken Salad. I hope you will give it a try. Really, kelp noodles are very good!

Makes 4 Servings

½ package Sea Tangle kelp noodles (6 oz.)

½ small head of green cabbage

½ bunch of green onions (about 4)

1 carrot

3 Tablespoons sugar

5 Tablespoons olive oil

½ teaspoon salt

6 Tablespoons white wine vinegar

¾ teaspoon pepper

¾ cup slivered almonds

⅓ cup dry roasted peanuts

15 oz canned premium white chunk chicken breast, drained

¼ cup chia seeds (optional)

Rinse the kelp noodles. Cut the noodles with scissors so they are more manageable to serve and eat.

Core the cabbage and then cut cabbage into small slivers. Chop the green onions. Grate the carrot. Mix the vegetables in a large bowl or (for really easy preparation and clean-up place in a 2.5 gallon zip top freezer bag) and stir.

In another container combine sugar, olive oil, salt, white vinegar and black pepper. Whisk to emulsify, this will take a couple of minutes. Pour the sauce onto the vegetable mix. Mix well. Let marinate for <u>4 hours</u> or so. Stir or knead bag every hour or so. Just before serving, add the nuts, the drained chicken and optional chia seeds, toss lightly.

* **For vegetarians, simply leave out the chicken**

Traditional Chinese Chicken Salad

For the person who desires the traditional recipe (without kelp noodles). Even if you like the Healthiest Chinese Chicken Salad, I hope you will give this recipe a try because it is one of my favorites!

Makes 4 Hearty Servings

> 2 packages Top Ramen Noodles
>
> ¾ to 1 small head green cabbage
>
> 1 bunch green onions (7 to 8 individual)
>
> 1 cup grated carrots (1 large carrot)
>
> 12.5 to 20 oz. canned chicken
>
> 6 Tablespoons sugar
>
> ¾ cup vegetable or olive oil
>
> 1 teaspoon salt
>
> ½ cup white wine vinegar
>
> 1 ½ teaspoon pepper
>
> ¾ cup slivered or sliced almonds

Core the cabbage and then cut cabbage into very thin slivers. Chop the green onion. Grate the carrot. Crunch the Top Ramen Noodles (with the noodles still in package, carefully hit the bags so that the noodles are broken into little pieces). Toss out the Top Ramen Noodles seasoning pack (too salty!). Mix the vegetables and crunched ramen noodles in a large bowl or (for really easy preparation and clean-up place vegetable and noodle mixture in a 2.5 gallon zip top freezer bag) and stir.

In another container, combine sugar, oil, salt, vinegar, and pepper and whisk briskly to emulsify, this will take a couple minutes. Toss together with the noodle vegetable mixture.

* **For vegetarians, simply leave out the chicken**

Chicken Verde Wrap

This is a variation of a recipe from "Camp Cooking WITHOUT Coolers II"

Makes 4 Servings

> 2 (10 oz.) cans of chicken breast, drained
>
> 4 oz. string cheese sticks (1 stick is about 1 oz) or try a big chunk to shred
>
> 2 (7 oz.) cans salsa verde (green salsa)
>
> 1 (7 oz.) can diced green chilies
>
> 8 (or so) Flatbread slices (Flatout brand is great)
>
> ½ small green cabbage
>
> 1 lime
>
> ½ Tablespoon sugar

Make the cabbage salad that is to be put inside wraps first. Slice cabbage thinly and place in a bowl. Squeeze lime over top of cabbage, add sugar and stir well (or for no mess mix up salad in a plastic bag).

Assemble wrap. Place about ¼ to ½ can of chicken in line down center of bread. Top with ¼ to ½ stick of string (or shredded) cheese, salsa, chilies and top with cabbage salad. Fold bread in half and eat like a taco.

* For a no-mess preparation and clean-up mix everything in a gallon size durable zip top freezer bag, otherwise prepare in a bowl.

Summer Lentils

For additional protein serve the summer lentils with salami and sardine topped crackers. Another good side for this dinner is fresh or dried fruit!

Makes 4 Servings

> 4 cups water
>
> 2 cups dehydrated lentils
>
> 3 Tablespoons dehydrated shallots
>
> 1 teaspoon minced garlic
>
> ¼ cup olive oil
>
> ¼ cup white wine vinegar
>
> ½ teaspoon ground cumin
>
> 1 teaspoon cayenne pepper
>
> 1 teaspoon salt

In a large bowl (or freezer bag), combine the water, lentils, shallots and garlic. Let rehydrate for half hour or so.

Drain the lentil mix until the liquid is completely gone. Add oil, vinegar and spices, stir well.

* For a no-mess preparation and easy clean-up, mix everything in a gallon size durable zip top freezer bag, otherwise prepare in a bowl.

Mango Couscous with Creamed Salmon

This is the no cooking version of a recipe from "Camp Cooking WITHOUT Coolers II"

Makes 8 Servings

Salmon Couscous

> ½ cup dehydrated mangos or apricots
>
> 6 Tablespoons dehydrated candied ginger
>
> 1 cup freeze-dried mangoes (about 2 oz.)
>
> 2 teaspoons powdered ginger
>
> 3 Tablespoons True Lemon (or 12 True Lemon 0.8g packets)
>
> 2 cups couscous
>
> 2 ½ cups water for couscous
>
> 20 to 24 oz. canned salmon
>
> ¾ cup cashew pieces

Dice the dehydrated fruit and candied ginger. Add the diced fruit and ginger to the 2 ½ cups of water. Stir in freeze-dried mangoes, ginger powder, True Lemon, cashews and couscous. Stir well to blend, cover and let rehydrate for an hour or two. It helps to place the couscous mixture in the sun or another warm spot.

Drain the salmon and add it to the couscous, stir lightly.

Sauce

>4 cups sour cream powder (16 oz. powdered)

>2 cups water

>1 ½ teaspoons ground cumin

>½ teaspoons salt

>½ teaspoons pepper

Rehydrate the sour cream powder with 2 cups of water. Add the cumin, salt and pepper. The longer the sauce sits the thicker it becomes. I usually thin it some by adding water a Tablespoon at a time.

To serve, top individual servings of couscous with sour cream sauce.

Southwest Smorgasbord

This is a versatile dish! You can serve it as a salad or wrap it up as a burrito (vegetarian option too)! Try it as a self serve burrito bar or smorgasbord style dinner.

Makes 4 Servings

Salad or Burrito Filling

>   1 (15-ounce) can corn kernels, drained
>
>   1 (14-ounce) can tomatillos, drained and chopped
>
>   1 (4-ounce) can diced green chilies, drained
>
>   2 (15-ounce) can pinto beans, drained
>
>   1or 2 limes, juiced
>
>   ½ teaspoon ground cumin
>
>   ½ teaspoon salt
>
>   ¼ teaspoon cayenne
>
>   3 Tablespoons olive oil
>
>   1 shallot, minced

Additional optional fillings for burritos

>   ½ head small green cabbage, shredded
>
>   1 small head of Romaine lettuce
>
>   1 or 2 (10 to 20 ounces) canned chicken
>
>   1 (7 ounce) can cheese (Bega brand)
>
>   1 can (7 ounce) Media Crema Table Cream

First make the burrito filling in a large bowl.

Prepare all the other optional fillings; shred cabbage, cut cheese, open cans of chicken and cheese. Lay out everything attractively on table. Everyone makes their own burritos.

Variation: Leave the beans out and you'll have a flavorful corn side dish.

DESSERTS

Marias Cookie Snacks

Sweet and Simple!

Makes 4 Servings

      5.5 oz. Marias Cookies

      1 small jar Nutella spread

      2 to 3 Bananas

Spread each cookie with about a Tablespoon of Nutella spread and top with 1 or 2 slices of banana. Make the whole package of cookies like this and then arrange attractively on plate to serve

   *   Marias Cookies - Gamesa is the best tasting brand.

Dutch Almond Dates

Dates are considered the oldest cultivated fruit in the world. Fossil evidence shows that date palms lived 50 million years ago. The fruit of the date palm has been cultivated for about 6,000 years in the Middle East. Dates are a staple part of many cultures' diets because of their nutritional value and easy portability.

Makes 4 To 6 Servings

> 16 large Medjool dates (use Medjool dates for best flavor)
>
> 4 ounces or so of almond paste
>
> ½ cup chocolate chips – chopped
>
> 16 whole almonds

Slice open dates and remove seed.

Knead or mix chopped up chocolate chips into almond paste. Roll filling mixture into a teaspoon size ball and place in date. Press a whole almond into the center of the date. Arrange nicely on a plate and serve.

Peach Leche Cake

Reminiscent of the Mexican "Tres Leches Cake" only a whole lot easier to make!

Prepackaged vanilla sweet bread or muffins

Canned Peaches or pineapple

Small container sweetened condensed milk

Lay out sweet bread in pan or serving plate. Layer fruit on top and pour sweetened condensed milk over the top. Serve immediately.

No-fuss Cherry Cheesecake

I have modified this box recipe so that it works well in the "no-coolers" kitchen. In order for it to set-up correctly, it is important to follow MY recipe directions, NOT the directions on the box.

Makes 6 To 8 Servings

> 1 (9 inch) ready-made graham pie crust
>
> 1 package Jell-O No Bake Cherry Cheesecake Dessert
>
> 3 heaping Tablespoons NIDO (dry whole milk powder)
>
> 1 cup water

Make the filling: Place powdered milk, filling mix, and water into a freezer bag. Squeeze out air as you carefully and securely zip the top closed. Knead for 3 minutes. Be careful as you knead the contents (you do not want the filling to be pushed out the top of the freezer bag).

Cut corner of baggie and squeeze filling into ready-made pie crust, filling the pie tin. Spread cherry topping on top.

Set up a "Bucket Refrigerator" so that the water is as cool as possible (see the description of a Bucket Refrigerator below). Place the cheesecake inside a large freezer bag and place in the "Bucket Refrigerator." Let cool and set for at least 15 minutes. Be very careful that the freezer bag is securely closed so that no water gets in to ruin the cheesecake.

BUCKET REFRIGERATOR

This is a system I use in place of a refrigerator (or cooler) to chill and allow desserts to set. It will require a large (1 or 2.5 gallon) locking freezer bag and 1 extra-large bucket or pan (I like the collapsible bucket sold by NRS called the "Big Basin Water Container" - see Resource Chapter for ordering information). You will also need a source of cool water such as a creek or river.

Step 1

Freezer bag and dessert

Step 2

Place dessert inside freezer bag and securely close the
top. Be sure no water can leak in through the top of the
bag.

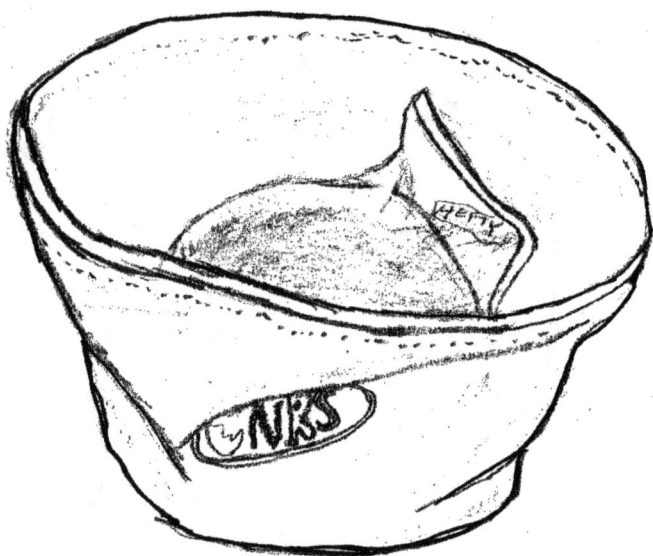

Step 3

Fill the bucket with cool water. Float the dessert (which has been placed inside the freezer bag) in cool water. Double check that the freezer bag is securely closed and that no water can get into the bag and ruin the dessert. Be sure the zip top of the freezer bag is not lying in the water.

Rum Balls

One of my favorite Christmas holiday treats, but good in the camp kitchen too!

Makes About 20 Balls

Balls

> ½ cup finely chopped walnuts or pecans
>
> 1 cup finely crushed vanilla wafers (Nilla Vanilla Wafer type)
>
> ¾ cup confectioners' sugar
>
> 1 Tablespoons cocoa powder
>
> ¼ teaspoon ground allspice
>
> ¼ cup dark rum
>
> 1 Tablespoon honey or light corn syrup (Karo Syrup)

Coating

> ½ cup finely chopped vanilla wafers

At Home: In a food processor first finely chop the walnuts and then separately process the 1 ½ cups of vanilla wafers. Place the chopped nuts and only 1 cup of the chopped wafers in a bag. Place the remaining ½ cup of chopped vanilla wafers in a different gallon size bag.

In Camp: In a large bowl, mix together ¾ cup of the confectioners' sugar, the cocoa powder and allspice. Stir in the rum and honey. Stir in the 1 cup of vanilla wafers and the chopped nuts then mix well.

Scoop out about ½ Tablespoon portion sizes of the chocolate mixture and roll into small balls. It is a good idea to wear gloves when using your hands for rolling the balls. Using your gloved hands, roll the balls in the baggie full of ½ cup of chopped vanilla wafers, coating evenly. Make one at a time rolling in the cookie crumbs remove from bag and set on plate to serve. If there are any left-over store in the bag of crushed cookie crumbs, preventing them from sticking together.

LOW-IMPACT CAMPING

Low-impact camping principles might not seem important until you consider the profound cumulative effect that thousands and even millions of visitors can have on a site over the years. One poorly located campsite or camp kitchen may have little significance, but thousands of such instances can do serious harm to our last wild environments and wildlife. Low-impact (Leave No Trace) camping seeks to minimize the changes we make just by visiting wilderness and other wild areas.

GUIDELINES FOR CAMPING

Kitchen Placement

Place the kitchen in previously used areas. When possible set up the kitchen on sand below the high water line rather than further compacting the earth and crushing vegetation higher up. I also recommend using a kitchen floor tarp. A kitchen floor tarp will catch the crumbs and scraps from the food preparation area (micro-trash). Doing this keeps the campsite cleaner so that it attracts fewer animals and insects.

Fires, Fire Pans, and Ashes

I like to say "no ash, no extra trash!" If you follow my no-cooking philosophy there is no impact from fires, at least for cooking! No fires or charcoal are needed for my recipes, so the mess and hassle of ash disposal is eliminated.

Trash – Pack Everything Out

Absolutely everything that came into the outdoors with you should go out with you except your urine and waste water. It is a good practice to have separate trash bags around the kitchen to keep recyclables separated from other garbage. This makes for easier clean up once you are home.

Purchase plastic compactor bags, burlap bags, and dry bags to contain trash. Place trash in plastic compactor bags. Place the plastic bag inside a burlap bag and keep the burlap wet with river water during your trip. This will slow decomposition and reduce the odor. When storing trash for the night or after the bag is full and needs to be carried on a boat, place the burlap-wrapped plastic bag in a dry bag for further protection. When packing up the kitchen for the night, the best place to store your trash away from critters is on your boat (be sure the bag is securely closed and burlap is wet). If you do not mind the extra weight, ammo cans and rocket boxes work well for storing trash and are critter resistant. For a lighter-weight, critter-resistant trash container, try a Vittle Vault (waterproof dry food container).

Strain Your Waste Water

Be sure to strain all waste water before disposing of it. One neat trick is to bring a bunch of panty-hose for this purpose. Get the large sizes! First, cut a pair apart to separate the two legs. Tie a knot about 6 to 8 inches down from the top of one leg, and snip the rest of the leg off just below the knot. Then spread the open end above the knot and pour the waste water into the panty-hose, over your catch bucket. Then toss that section of panty-hose into the garbage. Tie another knot and use a new section the next day. This is a cleaner approach than packing around a perpetually dirty metal or plastic strainer.

Disposal of Waste Water

The environment and the regulatory agencies determine the best method for disposal of waste water. Some agencies require that you spread it above the high-water line, while others want to see it poured into the river's current (not in an eddy, where it will swirl around endlessly or wash up on shore). In alpine regions the general rule is to disperse the waste water across the ground above the high-water line and, whenever possible, at least 200 feet from water sources and trails. In contrast, the desert river canyons cannot tolerate the waste water being disposed of on land because it rarely rains to flush and disperse contaminants into the soil. Know and follow the local rules.

Draining Oily Foods and Disposing of the Oil

Draining of tuna and other oily canned products presents a bit of a challenge. Oil and grease products should not go into the river nor should they be buried. Burying these materials will attract insects and animals. For proper disposal of small amounts of oil, soak up the oil with a paper towel and then toss the towel in the trash. For larger amounts of oil (or when draining tuna and other oily foods) drain into Tupperware type container and/or zip top bag and then toss that into the trash bag. The best way to avoid the oily mess is to purchase meats packed in water rather than oil.

Draining Non-Oily Foods

Keep a container/bucket half full of water in the kitchen during meal preparation just for draining the non-oily food products into. You can put stuff like pasta water, non-oily canned vegetable and fruit juice, liquid from canned beans, and leftover soda into the bucket and then dispose of it in the river (staining it of course). However, it needs to go into the current, so it does not wash up on shore.

ABOUT THE AUTHOR

Lacey is a veteran of the outdoors, having guided river rafters and backpackers all over the western United States and Mexico. Her decades of experience, both rafting and backpacking, provide her with a unique perspective on meal planning and allow her to create scrumptious meals that are low in bulk, lightweight, and nonperishable. The recipes provided here are only a sampling of the hundreds of meal ideas she has developed over the years. She is constantly refining and adding to her catalog of recipes in response to the inspiration, "Hey, I could make that in camp." A few years ago she began experimenting with new recipes using "raw foods" because many raw items will keep for several days without refrigeration and provide a tasty and nutritious alternative to processed foods. The result is this collection of recipes.

Lacey has also been profiled in Canoe & Kayak Magazine (May 2013) as one of the paddling community's "Covert Operators." She is the River Gypsy as described by staff writer Tyler Williams:

> When Lacey Anderson was held captive by an angry mob in farthest Guatemala, she came to a stunning epiphany. "I realized," she recalls, "that this could be my last day." For Lacey, the cold realization of mortality came with more irony than most. Lacey grew up in Southern California as a "wild child," she says; reared through the foggy lens of addiction, growing into another high school dropout. Fortunately, an innate connection with nature provided some peace. She read how-to books on camping and took her first backpacking

trip at sixteen. Nature's solace led her back to school where she earned a GED and a teaching degree, and eventually her own classroom of sixth graders. She had two daughters. Life went on.

Then, Lacey took a raft trip on the South Fork of the American. Her guide was female, and Lacey thought, "I can do this." A part time guiding career followed, both on rivers and trails, but it wasn't until her two daughters were grown and she tired of education's bureaucracy that Lacey redoubled her river interests and made it her life. Since 2009, Anderson has lived primarily out of her tricked-out Toyota camper truck, following runoff seasons from Idaho's snowmelt to Mexico's monsoon. In the extra cab of her truck rides a custom built SOTAR cataraft, perfect for the small and obscure rivers Anderson seeks.

Lacey's travels crossed paths with kayaker Rocky Contos a couple years ago, and the two have since completed over two dozen multi-day rivers throughout Mexico, from Sonora's Aros to Oaxaca's Atoyac. Several were first descents, not an endeavor normally suited to bulky rafts, but Anderson's extra small cataraft makes portaging a relative breeze, and she knows how to go light.

Several years ago while running support for kayakers on the Middle Fork of the Salmon (a river she regularly guides), Lacey organized impeccably gourmet meals without the use of a cooler. Her well-fed paddlers insisted that she publish the magic menu, and thus came Camp Cooking Without Coolers, a guide to tasty river meals attainable without burdensome blocks of ice. Her backpack boating style has helped Lacey go deep in search of jungle rivers like Guatemala's revered Copon, where her river-liberating film party was mistaken for corporate dam meddlers, and held at gunpoint while villagers threatened live immolation as punishment. Brave negotiations from the river parties' Guatemalan companions allowed Lacey her release, and she knew it wasn't her "last day," after all. It was just another life lesson, one she'll hopefully not have to employ on Peru's Maranon, a storied Amazon source river that Lacey hopes to row next winter. It's a long way from her Southern California roots, but for Lacey Anderson, maturing river gypsy, it's home.

THANK YOU

Thank you for your interest in my recipes, travel stories, and No Coolers blog **www.nocoolers.com**. Follow me on the blog to learn my secrets for planning, packing, and preparing delicious food on multi-day outings that don't require a cooler or ice. Check back frequently for tips, tricks, and new recipes. Be sure to keep an eye on my blog where I will be announcing the release date of my next cookbook.

Thank you for the purchase of this cookbook. You may be interested in my other cookbook titled "**Camp Cooking WITHOUT Coolers II Blueprint for using nonperishable food**" which includes a more extensive 7-day meal plan and lots more recipes. Many of the recipes are also "No Cooking." The recipes from that cookbook compliment the recipes in this book; in fact, I often refer to both when I am packing food for trips.

COMING SOON: Additional titles in the series:
Camp Without Coolers: Fresh & Healthy Vegetarian
Camp Without Coolers: Quick & Easy Vegetarian
Camp Without Coolers: The Nomadic Vegetarian
CWC: Grand Canyon, 3-Week Plan

www.ingramcontent.com/pod-product-compliance
Lightning Source LLC
Chambersburg PA
CBHW051432090426
42737CB00014B/2944